BOOKWORMS

Animal Homes

# A Squirrel's Hollow

Arthur Best

Cavendish Square
New York

Published in 2019 by Cavendish Square Publishing, LLC
243 5th Avenue, Suite 136, New York, NY 10016



First Edition



Website: cavendishsq.com



Library of Congress Cataloging-in-Publication Data

Names: Best, B. J., 1976- author.
Title: A squirrel's hollow / Arthur Best.
Description: First edition. | New York : Cavendish Square, 2019. |
Series: Animal homes | Audience: K to grade 2.
Identifiers: LCCN 2017055404 (print) | LCCN 2017057133 (ebook) |
ISBN 9781502636713 (ebook) | ISBN 9781502636706 (library bound : alk. paper) |
ISBN 9781502636720 (pbk. : alk. paper) | ISBN 9781502636737 (6 pack : alk. paper)
Subjects: LCSH: Squirrels--Nests--Juvenile literature. |
Squirrels--Behavior--Juvenile literature. | Animal behavior--Juvenile literature.
Classification: LCC QL737.R68 (ebook) | LCC QL737.R68 B47285 2019 (print) | DDC 599.36--dc23
LC record available at https://lccn.loc.gov/2017055404

Editorial Director: David McNamara
Copy Editor: Rebecca Rohan
Associate Art Director: Amy Greenan
Designer: Megan Metté
Production Coordinator: Karol Szymczuk
Photo Research: J8 Media

The photographs in this book are used by permission and through the courtesy of: Cover Skip Higgins/Raskal Photography/Alamy Stock Photo; p. 5 Oxygen/Moment/Getty Images; p. 7 Jim Nelson/Shutterstock.com; p. 9 Sandra Standbridge/Shutterstock.com; p. 11 David Prahl/Shutterstock.com; p. 13 Wolfgang Kaehler/LightRocket/Getty Images; p. 15 Gordon Wiltsie/National Geographic/Getty Images; p. 17 SpreewaldBirgit/Shutterstock.com; p. 19 Kenneth M. High ll/Science Source; p. 21 Sumio Harada/Minden Pictures/Getty Images.

Printed in the United States of America

# Contents

Squirrels are cute!

They live in many places.

Squirrels can be **gray**.

They can be brown.

They can be black.

Squirrels live near trees.

They eat fruit.

They eat nuts.

Squirrels live in trees.

A tree is a squirrel's home.

Squirrels can live inside trees.

They find a hole.

This is a **hollow**!

Squirrels also live on **branches**.

They live high up.

Squirrels make nests.

They use **twigs**.

They use leaves.

Nests keep squirrels safe.

Nests keep squirrels **warm**.

Squirrels have babies.

The babies live in nests.

They grow up.

They will live in a new tree!

# New Words

**branches** (BRAN-chez) Long sticks on a tree.

**gray** (GREY) Not quite black.

**hollow** (HAHL-oh) A hole.

**twigs** (TWIGZ) Small sticks.

**warm** (WARM) Not quite hot.

# Index

# About the Author

**Arthur Best** lives in Wisconsin with his wife and son. He has written many other books for children. Squirrels live in his backyard.

## About BOOKWORMS

Bookworms help independent readers gain reading confidence through high-frequency words, simple sentences, and strong picture/text support. Each book explores a concept that helps children relate what they read to the world they live in.